We Are Star Love

Lara Fairy Love Stockbridge

BookLeaf Publishing

Presentation by *BookLeaf Publishing*

Web: www.bookleafpub.com

E-mail: info@bookleafpub.com

ISBN: 9789357211963

First edition 2023

DEDICATION

To my Earth family for showing me my darkness!!!

To Wendy and Trev for Loving me ALLways!

To Holly and Lizzie for the same !

To Blue and Jake for growing in me and growing me !

To Coral awesome DDF

To AAAngel Josie you both know why!

To Angel Benjammin, Billie Rose ,ChrisTall, Nana Ivy and Granny Ethel

Always there keeping me connected!

To my Starfamily for shining bright!

So I see the pathways to Myself!

ACKNOWLEDGEMENT

When we need words we need them!

PREFACE

For All of Us!!!!!

Inspired by the Light and Dark in All of Us!

Forever Oneness who sings to Us in silence
Who teaches us through each other .
Guide my steps with strength and wisdom
and as I walk,
may I appreciate and learn
the lessons of each step.
Help me observe not judge.
Always speak from behind my eyes,
and let me do no harm.
But leave music and beauty after my visit.
and when I return to forever,
make the circle be complete
and the spiral be broader.

As We Will So It Is.

Anon

Still like Stars , homage to Maya Angelou

You could pull me down to misery,
With your ragged angry lines.
You may squash me in the stinking mud,
but still like Stars...I shine.

Does my Fairyness offend you?
Why are you stressed and sad?
Just cos I fly like I'm an Angel,
And I tapdance over bad.

Does my grief and loss offend you?
Why must I be like you?
I will continue to be myself
Caring less of what you do.

Just like Slugs and Spiders
And the range of nature's lines.
Just like Peace and Hope and Love
Still like stars ,
I shine!

The Lilith Family (sung to the tune of The Addams Family)

Love love love love (click fingers X2)
Love love love love (click fingers X2)
Love love love love
Love love love love
Love love love love(click fingers X2)

I am, you are, we are ,we.
I see, you see, we see, see.
I'm free, you're free, we're free, free.
We are reality.

Love love love love (click fingers X2)
Love love love love (click fingers X2)
Love love love love
Love love love love
Love love love love(click fingers X2)

I be , you be , we be , be.
I see, you see, we see, see.
I'm free, you're free, we're free, free.
Create reality

Love love love love (click fingers X2)
Love love love love (click fingers X2)
Love love love love
Love love love love
Love love love love(click fingers X2)

Compost 2

Waves of beauty and connection.
Pleasure piles.
Deep clefts and high peaks.
All beauty resounding.

In this darkened room duo.
sleep creates a solo.
Subconscious mind unwinds
Hoards of history ,
Hounding holy holding.

Violent beauty remoulding,
mouldy old pain and fear.
Long-forgotten now screaming,
ringing ears.

Body warm and soft ,
happy content,
leaning into pleasure places,
subconscious rises in phases.

Disgust and fear
Swirling here
No knowledge to allow,
the lovely into this now.

Feelings flayed like skin,
from a cat .
7 tails 7 times
grotesques gorging.
Lean in, allow the purging.

Elder takes youngers hand.
Leans into soft,
signals to this to is allowed,
welcomed, planned.

Releasing all old compounds
of terror pain and fear.

Allowing pure pleasure,
relenting and releasing ,
all that is no longer pleasing.

Stepping through old wars waged.
Releasing fears on to the page.
Letting go to learn and grow.
These tales make foundations,
for Star child to grow.

Twinkle Twinkle Shining Star. Sung to the tune of 'Twinkle ...

Twinkle Twinkle Shining Star.
Now I know You are my Heart.
Shining out my rays of Love
Connecting Heart , Below , Above.
Twinkle twinkle Shining Star.
Now I know you are my Heart.

When the blazing Sun was gone,
When the dark became my home.
Then you showed your little light,
Twinkle, twinkle, all the night.
Twinkle, twinkle, Shining star,
Now I know you are my Heart!
****
As the traveller in the dark,
I Thank you for your tiny spark,
Now I see which way to go,
My flaming heart , it twinkles so
Twinkle, twinkle, Shining star,
Now I know , you are my Heart.
****
In the dark blue sky you shine

Flaming Heart , forever mine
For you never shut your eye,
Till the sun is in the sky.
Twinkle, twinkle, shining star,
Now I know you are my Heart !
****
As your bright and tiny spark,
Lights this traveller in the dark,—
Now I know , just what you are
Twinkle, twinkle, shining star.
Twinkle, twinkle, Shining star,
Now I know you are my Heart !

I Am Apocalypse

At Samhain I stated,
I Apocalypse,it grated,
with all who have decided,
that thought is only two sided.

Apoco- away, Kalopsis-to cover
I'll state till it's clear,
I'm not trying to be clever.

The covers are off.
The shroud has been torn.
We now have awareness,
of why we've been born.

We are Heaven, we are Earth.
In imagination we create
what wishes to Birth.

Now freed from ridged bipolar Greek.
Now free from the interpolations of geeks.
My own interpolation, my own inserted text.
Is a revelation of Our Divinity
In all Life, Joy and Sex.

The glory of Now,

with no forced crucifixion.
The creation of reality,
With no electrical friction.

Belief in Self as the centre of All.
Free to think in spirals,
creating joyous sparks as we fall.

Our reality is Ours ,
throughout all we can play.
Creating each moment,
lighting Our own way.

It is easy and hard,
discerning what to disregard.
It is our Divine purpose,
to swim freely and worthless.

Stories are lights,
the mind to entertain.
Grains of a pile,
we step-by-step gain.

We are Life,we are Story.
We are Joy,we are Glory.
We are Love, we are Now.
Breathe deep and allow.

I am a Rainbow (Sung to the tune of I can see a Rainbow)

Red and orange and gold and green,
sky blue indigo white.
I am a rainbow I am a rainbow,
I am a rainbow light.

Red and orange and gold and green,
sky blue indigo white.
You are a rainbow you are a rainbow,
you are a rainbow light.

Listen with your eyes, listen with your eyes,
and sing everything you see.
I am a rainbow you are rainbow,
sing along with me.

Red and orange and gold and green,
sky blue indigo white
I am a rainbow, you are rainbow,
we are a rainbow light.

I am rainbow, you are rainbow
We are rainbow light

Treasure

What to share,
when having survived a nightmare.

Which stories are gems,
when all are glad,
none of it happened to them.

Which feelings to feel,
which scripts to put down,
finally process
and reveal.

We are Stardust.
We are Golden.
Which laws are defunct?
To which ones are we beholden?

To breathe deep now and let it pass.
Is the key to Our Now.
To which,
we do not,
have to bring,
the past!

Singing StarSongs heals us All (sung to the tune of ' Old MacDonald ')

Singing star songs heals us all.
SSSSS, HUUU, SHHHH, HAAAA,HOOO

And with this sound we heal our Lungs
SSSS, HUUU, SHHHH, HAAAA, HOOO

With a SSSSS here, and a SSSSS there.
Here a SSSSS, there a SSSSS.
Everywhere a SSSSSS, SSSSS.

Singing star songs heals us All.
SSSSS, HUUU, SHHHH, HAAAA,HOOOO.

Singing star songs heals us all.
SSSSS, HUUU, SHHHH, HAAAA,HOOOO.

And with this sound we heal our Kidneys
SSSS, HUUU, SHHHH, HAAAA, HOOO

With a HUUUU here, and a HUUUU there.
Here a HUUUU, there a HUUUU,

Everywhere a HUUUU HUUUU.

With a SSSSS here, and a SSSSS there.
Here a SSSSS, there a SSSSS.
Everywhere a SSSSSS, SSSSS.

Singing star songs heals us All.
SSSSS, HUUU, SHHHH, HAAAA, HOOO

Singing StarSongs heals us All.
SSSSS, HUUU, SHHHH, HAAAA, HUUUU.

And with this sound we heal our Liver
SSSS, HUUU, SHHHH, HAAAA, HOOO.

With a SHHH here, and a SHHH , there.
Here a SHHH there a SHHH,
Everywhere a SHHH, SHHH.

With a HUUUU here, and a HUUUU there.
Here a HUUUU, there a HUUUU,
Everywhere a HUUUU HUUUU.

With a SSSSS here, and a SSSSS there.
Here a SSSSS, there a SSSSS.
Everywhere a SSSSSS, SSSSS.

Singing star songs heals us All.
SSSSS, HUUU, SHHHH, HAAAA, HOOOO.

Singing star songs heals us All.
SSSSS, HUUU, SHHHH, HAAAA, HOOOO

And with this sound we heal our Hearts
SSSS, HUUU, SHHHH, HAAAA, HOOOOO.

With a HA HA here, and a HA HA there.
Here a HA there a HA .
Everywhere a HA HA

With a SHHH here, and a SHHH , there.
Here a SHHH there a SHHH,
Everywhere a SHHH, SHHH.

With a HUUUU here, and a HUUUU there.
Here a HUUUU, there a HUUUU,
Everywhere a HUUUU HUUUU.

With a SSSSS here, and a SSSSS there.
Here a SSSSS, there a SSSSS.
Everywhere a SSSSSS, SSSSS.

Singing star songs heals us All.
SSSSS, HUUU, SHHHH, HAAAA, HOOOO.

Singing StarSongs heals us All.
SSSSS, HUUU, SHHHH, HAAAA, HOOOO

And with this sound we heal our Spleen.
SSSS, HUUU, SHHHH, HAAAA, HOOO.

With a HOOO here and a HOOOO there
Here a HOOO, there a HOOO,
everywhere a HOOO HOOO.

With a HA HA here, and a HA HA there.
Here a HA there a HA .
Everywhere a HA HA

With a SHHH here, and a SHHH , there.
Here a SHHH there a SHHH,
Everywhere a SHHH, SHHH.

With a HUUUU here, and a HUUUU there.
Here a HUUUU, there a HUUUU,
Everywhere a HUUUU HUUUU.

With a SSSSS here, and a SSSSS there.
Here a SSSSS, there a SSSSS.
Everywhere a SSSSSS, SSSSS.

Singing StarSongs heals us ALL.
SSSS, HUUU, SHHH, HAAA, HOOO.

Revolution, Re- Loved Nation , for Lizzie Fairy!

The Rainbow is bright,
colours combining.
My Heart it is light,
Soul truth is shining.

A new time is begun,
a Nation is grieving.
This time is Our One,
Our Souls revealing.

The page it is blank,
this story not written.
Allow trust and give thanks.
Now ALL is forgiven.

Shine bright and heal well,
from stories before.
Walk straight out of Hell,
give a mighty roar.

Our time it is Now,
this we ALL write.
Breathe deep and allow.
Together WE shine bright.

Breathe

Breathe in....
allow, be.
Release, accept, grieve.

See your Light,
allow it to shine,
bright.

Feel, heal,
make joyous moments,
real.

Lean back,
Relax.
release emotions ,
That when boxed up,
inspire attack.

Get raw.
Get true.
Not with others,
but wordlessly within you.

Let the feeling finally Flow.
Sit on the Earth.
Feel connected, feel energised

From the Fire in the Belly
of She who Birthed Us.

Breathe out .....
Warming Body and Heart.
Heart opening,
warmth inspiring smiles.

Breathe in .....
Allow the joy,
to grow branches of Light
from Our head
and Our smiling faces
to our toes.

Sing for Joy.
Allow joyful resonance
in our Body and Soul.

Let Our ears ring,
with Our own joyous sound.

Breathe out .....
Allow Light to enter.
Allow Self to relax into ,
Oneness.
Being.
Peace.

Breathe in ....
Notice stories,
that call attention away,
from Oneness .

What seeks resolution?
What calls for attention?

Breathe out .....
Held in safety.

Allow the Story,
emotions,
feelings,
To be witnessed.

Breathe in ....
Allow darkness to brighten.
Allow Our load to be lightened.

Gently smoothed away,
as Sunrise follows Sunset.

The moment in-between
is where the Magic happens.

The Sun is rising.
Be the Light!

Breathe out.....

Release

Heat.
Heart, healing.
Rolling, reeling, feeling.

Tides rise, open eyes.
Giving room, to flumes.

Oceans of emotions.
Cracked but not broken.

A spiral story.
A continuous curve.

Trust and step up.
Prove we have nerve.

Sex ,Death and Gardening

Gardening,
is all about,
Sex and Death.
He said.

Now,
the garden grows,
and,
He is dead.

Another look,
shows me,
clearly.
That he never died.
Not really.

The sweetness of the marjoram.
The bluntness of the Sage.
The bitter of the Mugwort
Chamomile calming rage.

He is alive,
forever.
The plants.
His Heart.

His hands.

As we,
grow forever,
fuller.

Humanities,
healing,
Lands

Full Moon Eclipse Star Transmission

At this time of dark and light,
laugh.
All is well
Make more light.

Trust our Heart.
Receive boundless Love.
Feel our Joy.
Fly with doves.

Accepting Love,
Soul song resounding.
Here below and above
The mission bell sounding.

Liberation focusses.
Awakens fascination.
Exquisite Joy opens.
Focusing liberation.

Now free from all past histories.
Stepping fearless into Reality.
Rainbow purpose brightly shining.
Words thoughts and actions,

All combining.

Remember purpose.
Remember joy.
Shining bright.
Beings Girls and boys.

Transmuting darkness to light.
Forgiveness is key.
Bring Our Rainbow flame forward,
Lightening density.

Transparency liberates.
Integrity fascinates.
Accountability opens.
Lovelight resonates.

Forgive and have fun.
All chords dissolving.
We are all one.
Our Soul still evolving.

Release suffering,
to Our Star Families,
who rejoice in the holding.
We are All One.
Our Planet evolving.

Birthing true vision,

of Our,
'All we would Love to be' mission.
Imagination powering,
Quantum cell frisson.

Emotion is motion.
Love is a verb.
Frequency is everything.
Vibrate beyond words.

We are Soul
We are Glory.
We are Light.
We are Love.

Be at Peace.
Transmit joy.
Heart,
here,
below,
and above.

I Am a Chalice

Regardless,
of what 1970s childhood ,
Eastenders , Home and Away, and Neighbours,
taught me.

I Am a Chalice,
open and free.

Despite unconsciously learning ,
I was negative criticism,
emotions and greed,

I am a Sacred Mind,
Reverental and free.

Forgetting school rules ,
gender and bias.

I Am a rising tide of Love.

Free and fearless.

Life....Death ...Life

Dying is always necessary before renewal.

Death and dying are commonplace.

However we still wail.

Death is the beginning.
Death Is the end.
Death is our enemy.
Death is our friend.

Our life leads to Death,
in the blink of an eye.
Pay attention, make space.
Discuss how we die.

Life becomes vibrant,
Life gains meaning.
Life dances with Death,
every time there is feeling.

Life lives and grows.
Death creates compost.
Life reminding Us All,

When we Love,

We,
are,
never,
lost.

The day after

The day after,
the anniversary of the fall ,
of the Berlin wall.

We accept mercy.
We trumpet Our call.

Angelic army disbanded.
Now Humans One and All .
Realising and relating,
as We process,
and We fall.

Star beings truly Earthed.
Flighty light, physically grounded.
Starlight lighting darkness,
ragged, broken, hounded.

Heroes, Heras , travellers All.
free to experience,
Fire, Water Steam
Transition point revelations,
shining stars as We fall.

Open to it All ,

Crystal boundaries shining.
Allowing yes and no.
Individuality defining.

Laughing joyous hymns.
Releasing fear and sorrow.
Beings, Hers and Hims ,
Creating bright tomorrow's

Demonically Angelic

How can we mobilise emotion,
to open us to Divine devotion ?

How can we feel the feels,
and let them guide us to what is real ?

How can We get past this?
How do We smash the wall?
How do We fly as Angels
while still aware,
of Our fall?

Divine dichotomy
Desire, Dread and Death.
Whore, whole and holy ,
strangled of our breath .

Dancing wider.
Laughing stronger.
Joking harder.
Giggling longer.

Widening the whelming,
laugh, dance, roll.

Allowing the joke ,
to remake Us Whole

Flow and Glory

Smooth,
Gliding through,
essential essence resounding.

Recognise what's true,
allow roots
allow grounding.

Wishes widening whelming.
Heart gently opening.
Telling tales worth telling.
New light and life opening.

Crystal light shining ,
old emotions fully cleared
New stories now defining.
Creating magic weaving weird

Glory

Excitement and fear.
Emotions that both feel queer.

Bile rises,
is it really?

Crying and laughing ,
nearly !
Allowing and boundaried,
in control and now free.

Initiation into creation,
Deep wishes now freed.

Allowing Peace.
Allowing Love
Allowing Joy.
Allowing story .

Opening to the Rainbow Flame of Now
Resplendently
We glory!

I. I Am .

I didn't even know who I was ,
until I began to learn,
to Love myself as I am.
In this very moment.
.
I thought I was my thoughts.
The runaway Train,
of dislike disapproval and disgust.

I now call ,
on my Ancestral Powers ,
of my train driver Grandfather's
Richard and Albert.

I drive my own train
powered by my Divine ability
to Love and approve of myself.

I am perfect as I am.
and all I have I share.
I know We Are All One
and there is enough.

I Shine,
I Share

I Love .

I Am (can be sung to the Stray cat Strut baseline)

I Am All that is
I Am All that is
I Am All that is

I am the source of All of my creations

I am the Source of All of my situations

I Am Divine Love
I Am Divine Light
I Am Divine Peace

I Am Divine Masculine
I Am Divine Feminine
I Am Divine Child

I Am Divine Trust
I Am Divine Joy

I Am a Multidimensional Being
Of Synthesis and Fusion

I Am Divine Truth

I Feel Divine Anger
I Feel Divine Pain
I Feel Divine Fear
and I Feel Divine Rage

I Feel Divine Jealousy
I Feel Divine Lust
I Feel Divine Hate
And I Feel Divine Mistrust

I'm All these things
I'm Black and White

And their Sysygy within,
Shines my Being Loving Rainbow Light

I respect and walk My path

And as I walk I know
You'll hear me Laugh

Because I and Divine Love
I Am Divine Light

Cos I Am All That I Am

I Am That I Am

I Am That I Am

Oh , I Am That I Am

Oh I Am Divine Love
I Am Divine Light
I Am Divine
I Am
I

Compost

What does a compost bin
look like just before it's cleaned?
Someone else's job ?
disgusting, dirty degolas.

A shameful mess.
The leftovers and dross.
The stuff you want to,
just get lost .

Now see the cleaned bin,
shiny, new, clear and clean.
wiped clean of the ming,
that's always bin.

Apply to self,
and witness it wholly.
Know both states are truly Holy.

The flux and flow,
the emptiness, the full.
creates what is known,
relates the Star pull.

Holy and whole.

Empty and pure.
Joyously falling,
Love will endure.

Gatheration

Some of this simply don't know better.
Some of us are still asleep.
When we know better, we do better.
Old floors of memory we sweep.

Tales of today and yesterday,
are clearly all the same.
The micro-macro loving acts,
Through compassion Our Souls we regain.

Reality as we have been taught it,
has little to do with reality as it is.
Science quantum links bits,
recognising ALL is part of what is .

One essence manifesting individually,
dancing Tangos throughout time .
Spiritual beings manifesting physically.
Compassion creating stars that shine.

Right now Our eyes are opening .

RIght now we are beginning to see.
Our individual Oneness Shining
We are All as a wave is to the sea.

www.ingramcontent.com/pod-product-compliance
Lightning Source LLC
Chambersburg PA
CBHW051740130826
49812CB00033B/934